The What Now Mindset

Volume 1

Presented by
WNM Ventures, LLC

DEDICATION

This book is dedicated to all of the entrepreneurs, business owners, career professionals and other individuals who have had to pivot and say, "What Now".

FOREWORD

How is it that two people can experience the same setback but have different responses?

For example, two people can get fired from their job. One person responds by starting their dream business while the other sinks into depression and despair.

Two business owners can experience the same global pandemic. One will make strategic pivots, while the other will stop planning and just wait until things "get back to normal."

These tendencies are a part of what inspired Dr. Sharon H. Porter, Ted Fells, and I, to start The What Now Movement, and to create this book, The What Now Mindset.

Our mission is to help people to pivot in a positive direction when they face a crisis that leaves them asking, "What Now?"

My two co-founders and I faced one of these moments back in January of 2020.

We were planning to join forces to create in person summits that would be hosted in hotel conference rooms around the world.

We had envisioned thousands of people packed in a room, acquiring knowledge that would shift their business and change their life.

What we didn't envision, was a Covid 19 pandemic shutting down all in- person events and gatherings.

We were faced with a crisis that left us asking, "What Now?"

This experience combined with the growing number of people who told us they were "waiting for things to get back to normal", led to the creation of The What Now Movement.

After conducting over 28,000 coaching sessions with entrepreneurs and executive leaders, I have discovered that your mindset is what determines how you respond to life's "what now moments."

You can't have an effective response without first embracing the right mentality.

Which is why we are so glad that you have picked up a copy of this book, The What Now Mindset.

The stories shared by the nine featured women, are all What Now moments, that will inspire you to embrace the right mentality and make pivots that keep you on course with your life's purpose.

Many of the stories are personal stories acknowledging their work, life, and all things are intertwined.

Themes of grief, faith, family, inner strength, love, pain into purpose, gratitude, patience, kindness, mental health, well-being, and service of others, are threaded throughout the pages.

As I previously noted, my co-founders and I were forced to ask, "What now?"

The book you are holding in your hands represents the answer to our question.

What is the answer to your "what now" question?

Eric M. Twiggs

President & CEO of The What Now Movement

http://thewhatnowmovement.com/

CONTENTS

ACKNOWLEDGMENTS

The What Now Movement and WNM Ventures, LLC would like to acknowledge the contributing authors for sharing their What Now Journeys.

Thank you:

Lori Blatt

Carly Bressler-Archambeau

Laurie G. Curtis

Steph Annie Cutler

Leslie Grodin

Janna Holcomb

Trina Holman

Kristin Murner

Xavier Whitford

We would also like to thank, Dawn Marie Bornheimer for managing this project.

INTRODUCTION

"What we plan for ourselves isn't always what life has planned for us"

What Now? is a question the majority of individuals, families, and business owners have had to ask in the last two and half years. The COVID-19 Pandemic stopped many in their tracks. Those who took a pause and chose to pivot found a new way of doing things, a new way of thinking, a different mindset. Psychologist and author, Dr. Carol Dweck, has identified two mindsets, the Fixed Mindset and the Growth Mindset. You may also be familiar with a Positive Mindset, an Abundance Mindset, and even a Goal-Setting Mindset. In this book collaboration, we would like to introduce the *What Now Mindset*. Your mindset is how you see the world around you; it is your way of thinking. Your mindset determines your responses to circumstances, events, and situations.

The What Now Movement had an opportunity to share space with several individuals over the past two and half years who experienced a "What Now Moment", some more than one moment.

We spoke with **April Lewis**, who is an army veteran and Certified Health Coach. Her *"What Now Moment"*, came on February 27, 2006, when she received a phone call informing her that her husband of three years had been killed in Iraq. She realized her life would never be the same. This was the first time she had experienced grief. She first became angry and the anger manifested into depression, substance abuse, and suicidal thoughts and behavior. She says she lost her mind, but gained her voice. She realized healing for her came through sharing her story. The What Now Mindset for April was to "Seek Happiness".

Genesis Amaris Kemp, author, podcast host, and DEI Consultant, shares that she received continuous "Nos" in the workplace. No to promotions, no to moving from administrative (admin) positions to professional positions, although she was qualified. There were no advocates or sponsors to assist her in navigating the corporate space. She realized she had to become her own advocate and champion for where she wanted to go. She became the driving force in her own career trajectory. Genesis worked in the oil and gas industry, a majority white male industry. Oftentimes, she would be the only woman or the only woman of color. She refused to let those barriers prevent her from moving ahead in the industry. To adapt she began seeking informal mentors, journaling to get her thoughts on paper, and continuously prayed. Her *"What Now Moment",* was after a performance review with her supervisor. Throughout the review, she was led to believe that her ranking would increase. She was ranked as a "B" and felt it should have been an "A". In addition, she was being paid as an admin, but doing the work of a professional. It was during that day and in that season, she realized there was more that God wanted her to do and that this was the time to come up with her 3 Rs: Refuel, Refocus, and Realign.

Ash Shukla, Founder of Financial CHAKRAS™, arrived with his family in the United States from India on September 4, 1989. They were a low-to middle class family and the first in the family to migrate to the U. S. No one in the family spoke English. The family only had their passports. Ash was the first one in the family to get a job. He walked three miles there and back in addition to going to school. Despite all of the challenges they experienced, one thing they knew for sure was that they were going to make it. With hard work and dedication, in one year, Ash had accumulated about $20,000, and the family purchased a home. Ash graduated from high school and was now enrolled in college, majoring in computer science and was introduced to the financial field. He worked for Citibank, Sunstrust, and PNC. Initially, he was not good at sales. He had to take the Insurance exam eight times before he passed. English as a second language was a significant hurdle, but he never looked at it as a failure. He saw it as a step-forward. Tenacity and the ability to persist is how he was able to move forward during his *"What Now Moment"*. Failure was not an option. The only option was to succeed.

Kyonna F. Brown, the Forgiveness Expert, struggles started with youth obesity and resenting her parents for being raised by her grandparents. Her parents were using drugs, her father was in and out of prison. Her mother would eventually spend time in the prison system as well. She started smoking marijuana and hanging with friends that were breaking the law (i.e. stealing cars).

As a result of broken relationships, she sought attention, any attention.

She wanted to escape her reality. Attention came from another woman. That relationship eventually led her to serving prison time for being the getaway driver, while this person, who she felt loved her, robbed a store.

Kyonna says, "Forgiveness was the catalyst that allowed me to operate into a destiny." The biggest component was forgiving herself.

In July of 1990, at the age of 13, **Aaron Graves,** the first African-American head baseball coach at Riverdale Baptist, in Upper Marlboro, MD, had a bad headache, so much so, his parents rushed him to Southern Maryland Hospital in Clinton, Maryland. He received a CT Scan and was then medevaced to Children's Hospital in Washington, DC. He would have several more tests before being admitted. It was determined that he had a mass on the base of his brain. A doctor that was flown in from Madison, Wisconsin, told him that if he didn't have the surgery he would die. Hearing this prognosis, all Aaron could think about was that all of his aspirations of playing high school and college football and baseball was just diminished. He wanted to give up. He didn't even want to have the surgery, he didn't want to live. His surgery was scheduled for July 30, his father's birthday was July 29 so they celebrated both his father's birthday and his life with a cookout. He went in for surgery the next morning, while under anesthesia, he had a vivid dream of bright white clouds. As he was walking towards a large golden gate, he sees two individuals standing there.. The gate opens and he sees his Uncle Jason that passed from a car accident very shortly after his high school graduation. The other person was his great-grandfather. Both of them were wearing familiar items. The moments that follow, the imagery goes black and he wakes up in the ICU. The doctor shares with him that he had to be revived and that he was clinically dead for 1 minute and 47 seconds. He had to relearn to walk, talk, and use his motor skills. The doctor also informed him that he could no longer play contact sports.

Aaron's first *"What Now Moment"* was at the age of 16, he realized he was getting ready to go to college and still learning how to deal with not being a "normal teenager". The next "What Now Moment" was in college, at the end of his sophomore year, when he was kicked out of college because of his grades. His father gave him two options: Figure out how to get back into school or go out on his own. He has had to figure out *"What Now"*, throughout his life.

We thank April Lewis, Genesis Amaris Kemp, Ash Shukla, Kyonna F. Brown, and Aaron Graves, for sharing some of their most vulnerable moments.

In this book collaboration, nine authors share in their own words, their What Now Moments and how a *What Now Mindset* helped shift their circumstances.

Trina Holman

CHAPTER

HOLDING TOGETHER

By Trina Holman

In 2021, I faced the greatest test of my life. Through it, I discovered that while not all challenges can be solved, we have a responsibility to choose growth even in our most trying times.

I am generally pretty resourceful at finding creative solutions.

Like many, when the pandemic hit, I found new problems to figure out. My work involved frequent travel and many face-to-face meetings. How would I work now?

As an extrovert, I thrived on interaction with others and a quick pace to life. How would I manage staying at home every day?

Would my husband Lance and I enjoy spending so much time together? He was already a pro at working from home. He'd had a home office for six months already and his routine was pretty set.

It took a while, but I slowly created a space that worked. I found the missing connection with people by visiting with old and new friends over Zoom. We were mindful of what was going on in the world but not consumed by it. Family celebrations continued, even if gathering together was much different than we would have liked.

Days spent at home also meant the gift of time to focus on our relationship and our health.

Time together was good.

We both made great progress.

My husband, in a wheelchair from injuries due to a car accident, was well on his way to reach the health goal needed to receive double knee replacements. He would finally be able to walk again. He lost 150 pounds, no longer needed insulin, and reduced his blood pressure medicine. He worked hard to reach his goals. He felt good. The best he'd felt in many years.

We allowed ourselves to dream again.

Our four kids were grown. We made plans to buy an RV, work remotely and travel together.

Life was feeling pretty promising even in the middle of a pandemic.

Those dreams were put on hold with the sudden death of my mother-in-law in July of 2021. A whirlwind of grief overcame our family. The kids were especially close to their grandmother having spent most of their summers with her. We grieved together as a family as we reminisced over photos and pilfered through many boxes of memories in her home.

As hard as it was, it was so good to be together. Joy seeped through the tears because we thrived in our togetherness.

Everyone handles grief differently, but the support of a close family made it more bearable for us. We chose to celebrate life and great memories at the funeral. As an only child, my husband began taking care of closing out his mother's estate. The pain was raw, everyone was exhausted, but our family was recovering together.

Less than a month later, a positive Covid-19 test for both of us changed everything. The physician at the walk-in clinic told my husband to go to the emergency room, his blood oxygen levels were low. He balked at the idea, but we expected he would receive some oxygen to help and be sent home. He was tired yet felt good, and strong. Pandemic protocols and my own infection meant I could not enter the ER with him. I unloaded the wheelchair, pushed him to the automatic door and kissed him goodbye.

"I'll call you when I'm ready to come home," he said.

He didn't come home.

He was admitted. No visitors allowed.

I recovered at home, alone.

Communication was sometimes problematic because neither of us had much energy. We talked on the phone as much as possible, sometimes just sitting in silence together.

Some days I would send photos of Lance's dog Ronon being goofy or looking sad missing his "Pops" being there to play ball. A blue heeler,

Ronon came to the family one year earlier. Lance had Non-Hodgkin's Lymphoma from 2018-2019; adding Ronon to the family was part of celebrating clear scans that meant the end of chemo for Lance. They quickly became best buds. I hoped those photos would give him a smile and more drive to recover.

A week into the hospital stay for Covid-19 recovery, Lance's oxygen levels were holding steady even if not improving. Rest was good; movement stressed his lungs. To give the lungs a boost, continuous positive airway pressure (CPAP) therapy was prescribed. He still sounded strong even through the forced air.

We remained confident he would be home soon and planned our next day trip. We dreamed together through texts about our first destinations when we bought our RV.

One night Lance called. He was incredibly stressed.

He spoke through labored breath and broken sentences. The nurses tried to get him out of bed, but it did not go well.

The problem was that there had been no intake interview on admission. The care team did not have Lance's history. They were unaware that his legs did not work and pushed him to "try," thinking he was just not making the effort. Lance's oxygen levels dropped significantly; his heart rate accelerated. The nurses rushed into action taking measures to get him back in bed to regulate the heart.

I asked, "Are you okay?"

He only said, "I don't know… I have to go."

Those were the last words I heard him speak.

Lance was placed on a ventilator that night.

I knew this wasn't good and fell to the floor. The pain and fear of losing him poured out of me in gut-wrenching screams that came from deep within my soul. It was as if a part of my heart was being ripped from my chest.

I believe now that I began grieving at that moment even without knowing it consciously.

We had a problem.

Extra stress was put on Lance's already weak body because the care team did not have his medical history and other crucial information to his healing.

His care team also needed to understand he was more than a patient. He was a deeply loved father, husband, and soon-to-be grandfather.

The next day, our girls and I delivered photos for the nurses to put up in his room.

I wrote a list of all the important things about him to tape to the wall.

Every night following, the kids and I called Lance's phone on a conference call.

A nurse would place the phone by his ear. We would talk to him, pray over him, tell him how much we loved him, believed in him, and needed him. We sometimes played his favorite music.

An avid Arkansas Razorback football fan, we provided score updates and we even "called the Hogs." That beloved battle cry wasn't just for the football team.

Although the calls helped us feel more together, physical isolation remained a major problem for both of us.

Our hearts and souls were connected.

We needed to see, hear, feel, and touch each other in order to heal.

Twenty-one days after his symptoms began, I was finally allowed to visit. I spent one full day sitting with him, holding his hand, brushing his hair, and having long one-sided conversations about everything I could think of. We had so many dreams to plan.

I still believed he would come out of it. This problem too would be solved.

Lance beat every obstacle ever placed in his path.

The reports from the doctors were promising. His kidney function returned to a normal range. His lungs had cleared. Even those problems were solved.

Two of our kids were able to see him the following days.

And we felt hopeful ... until the very next night.

The phone rang.

The hospital was calling.

The nurse said I should come immediately.

I didn't quite understand.

Protocol said only one person would be allowed. That was not acceptable. The family needed to be together. To be there with him. Lance needed us there. I pleaded. I knew then that he would be leaving us soon.

They quietly allowed our family to gather around him.

We prayed. We told him we loved him, and it was okay to let go.

We said goodbye, for now. Only our faith in God was holding us up.

> "For our light and momentary troubles are achieving for us an eternal glory that far outweighs them all. So, we fix our eyes not on what is seen, but on what is unseen, since what is seen is temporary, but what is unseen is eternal."

2 Corinthians 4:17-18

Throughout this entire time, we had a strong network of prayer warriors.

I borrowed their strength to physically heal from Covid. I borrow their strength still today as I continue to grieve our seemingly insurmountable loss. The house is empty, but my heart is not.

Most couples will eventually face the loss of a spouse. That part is not unique.

However, Covid widows represent a snapshot in time, an unprecedented event in recent history. Too many never had the chance to say goodbye;

their loved one died alone.

Even as grief continues to assault my mind, I am eternally grateful to have held Lance's hand as he departed his body for complete healing and eternal glory.

I grieve also for the many families who did not have the same opportunity to say goodbye. Their grief and recovery are even more of a challenge.

Grief is an ongoing process that never quite completes. This is a problem I cannot solve but I can heal.

We fortified our hearts with a quote recently overheard.-"We will never be whole again, but we won't always be broken."

It was time to begin healing. There was no choice in the suffering that came to our family. However, now I have a responsibility to choose how I respond. It's my decision.

So I choose how I move forward.

I choose how I honor the legacy of my husband.

I choose not to live in pain. Lance would not want me to.

I choose to live now for the life we had, for the four beautiful lives we made, for the love we shared.

Still, the choice to move forward is easier than the action. It presents a new problem in resilience. How *does* one move forward when the carpet of life is pulled out from under them?

It takes extraordinary effort every single day. The good news is that resilience is not extraordinary. It is an empowered response to life.

As I continue to mourn losing the love of my life, I choose to hold tight to what is beyond my understanding.

In faith, I move forward. In growth, I discover who I am now and who I am called to serve as I live out my purpose.

ABOUT
TRINA HOLMAN

Trina Holman is a personal development consultant and president of The TK Holman Company.

She specializes in empowering women to take the lead for their self-development including personal safety. Her signature programs help individuals and teams find their comparative strengths through discovering the power of choice.

Trina is a DISC Personality Indicator certified behavioral trainer. She is a member of the Maxwell Leadership Certified Team, the Association of ESD Professionals (Empowerment Self Defense), the American Writers & Artists Institute, and the Professional Writers Alliance. She holds a bachelor of science in Organizational Management from John Brown University.

Mother to four grown children and a new grand-daughter, Trina's heart is most full when her whole family is around the table together. She loves travel and taking the roads less traveled but it is the beautiful lakes and trails around Northwest Arkansas where she spends as much time as possible, usually either hiking or kayaking. Her blue heeler, Ronon Dex likes to tag along but mostly loves road trips, especially if he gets a pup cup on the way home.

Janna Holcomb

CHAPTER

MORE THAN MEETS THE EYE

by Janna Holcomb

Human connection is essential to our existence. Some connect through deep conversation, others by physical touch or a shared experience. What would you do if your preferred means of connection were suddenly taken from you? Sharing energy with another person through eye contact is a gift I took for granted my entire life. That is, until I lost it.

Strabismus

In 2019, after two pregnancies in as many years, accompanied by progressive and unexplained vision loss in my right eye, doctors discovered a tumor pressing against my optic nerve and brain. The decision was quickly made to operate and try to remove as much of it as possible, as they wouldn't discover until after surgery that the tumor was noncancerous.

I awoke from my craniotomy, and immediately knew something was vastly different and wrong with my vision. I was dizzy and saw two of everything. It took only a few minutes to comprehend what had happened -- I was cross-eyed.

During my pre-operative meeting with the ophthalmologist, she had outlined all possible risks of the surgery. One of these was that my right eye might no longer align with my left. I begged my doctor to do everything she could to prevent me from having misaligned eyes, or strabismus.

As it turned out, this is precisely what happened.

In the ICU, during my first post-surgery consultation, one of the ophthalmologists explained what had occurred. My tumor wasn't a solid mass, but a fleshy, stringy thing, similar in texture and color to the muscles and flesh surrounding it. Removing it from behind my eye was particularly challenging, as it was difficult to tell what was part of the tumor and what was not. The surgeon had inadvertently damaged a nerve, leaving one of my eye muscles paralyzed.

A quick anatomy lesson: the eye has four main muscles that contribute to movement, located on the right, left, top, and bottom. Each muscle has an equal amount of tension on the eye, so if one stops working, its opposite muscle pulls too much, and the eye no longer rests in the center position. Essentially, paralysis of the eye muscle closest to my right ear meant there was nothing pulling my eye taut and to the right, leaving the muscle closest to my nose to do all the pulling. Thus, my right eye gazed over the bridge of my nose in the resting position, while my left eye looked straight ahead. To save me from dizzying double vision, I was given a stack of self-adhesive eye patches to cover my right eye. I started wearing these the day of my surgery. I didn't imagine I would end up wearing them for months.

I recovered well from the surgery and started to get used to the new shape of my head. In addition to the large c-shaped scar from the craniotomy and a bit of missing hair, titanium mesh supports the skin at my temple, where bone used to be. This area has become sunken in over time, and the bone below bulges unnaturally. Above the end of my right eyebrow, bumps from a row of screws can be seen, if you look closely enough. I also have a strange vertical indentation on the right side of my forehead which leads up to my incision scar. There is no explanation for this feature, but I like to joke that when they put Humpty Dumpty back together again, perhaps they forgot a piece.

Are You Looking at Me?

Though stark, none of these visible changes in the structure of my face could compare to the fact that my eyes no longer aligned. I adjusted slowly to the double vision, undoubtedly aided by the lack of improving vision in my right eye. My brain learned to cancel out what my right eye communicated to it.

Despite my ability to overcome the vision-related challenges of strabismus, I was still unable to overcome the *visible* ones. Frankly, I was embarrassed by my eyes, and my self-confidence took a nosedive the months following the surgery. The embarrassment was profound enough that I wore an eye patch every time I went out in public for the first two months. I didn't do this because I needed to, or because it helped me focus better while driving. I wore a patch because I was ashamed of the inability to make eye contact with people using *both* of my eyes. I feared the lack of eye contact would distract them or make them uncomfortable. At least with an eye patch, I thought, maybe they'd believe my eye was injured, and not that I had a creepy eye staring over their shoulder and off into space.

I worried if they saw my eyes, people would wonder about my intellect. This fear may sound strange. I have thought about it in the years since, and there may be good reason to worry. After all, in our culture—through TV, films, and social media, people with misaligned eyes are frequently the butt of jokes, portrayed as mentally handicapped, or made to be the villain.

Owning My Worth

I eventually returned to my job at the Pentagon, and I left the patches at home. I decided to follow the firm, but loving, advice from my boss's wife, "Just own it, Janna!" I was scared, not so much of interactions with folks who already knew me and worked with me, but of the people I had yet to meet. The people who didn't know me *before*. I had an important job working for a high-profile military leader, and I interacted with my counterparts and other military leaders daily. *What would they think of me?* Eventually, I had to let go of this fear as much as I could and did my best at owning my crossed eyes.

Shortly after my craniotomy, I met with an ophthalmologist who specializes in strabismus. Four and a half months after the initial surgery and damage to my eye muscle, I had my first strabismus surgery which involved a complex plan to detach, divide, and otherwise move other eye muscles to reach my main goal of having my right eye centered when at rest. The surgery was quite successful, and after six weeks of healing, the goal was met. I still required a second strabismus surgery six months later, for a slight tweak of the previous work.

To say I'm totally satisfied with the outcome would be inaccurate. I'm incredibly pleased I can now look at people with both eyes, but it still takes effort to focus completely on what is in front of me. My right eye tends to wander, and the primary gaze (looking straight ahead) is the only angle in which I do not have severe double vision. A consequence of strabismus that had never occurred to me until I actually experienced it is the absence of depth perception. Even after the corrective surgeries, I frequently reach for cabinet knobs or drawer handles, only to miss on the first try.

Another significant change for me is when I see a person with strabismus, I now go out of my way to look at them unwaveringly in the eye that is looking back at me, and I smile. I am kind—maybe too kind— because I know so many people with this condition are discriminated against, looked upon as less-than, and experience things that most others cannot conceive of. But I can. If only for a short time, I walked in their shoes as a person with a *visible* condition that affects our everyday lives. I still have strabismus today, but I am fortunate to be able to hide it much of the time. There are so many who don't have this privilege.

The realm of self-worth has never been my strong suit, even before this experience, so having a significant change to my appearance was hard for me. What bothered me most was I felt I could not connect with people if I couldn't look at them with both eyes. What I have learned is, my worth is not tied to whether or not I can look someone in the eye. No one's worth is. I am able now to look beyond face value and recognize we all have seen and unseen struggles. We all deserve to feel a sense of belonging, to be respected, valued, and treated with kindness.

Today, gratitude is an intentional practice for me. I am grateful the tumor wasn't life-threatening, and that I still have good vision in one of my eyes. I am grateful for a loving and supportive husband, who has stood by me every step of the way, and for my two amazing daughters. I'm grateful to still serve in the military today, and I've been allowed to continue my duty despite some challenges. I'm grateful that, while the image looking back at me in the mirror is different than I thought it would be, this experience has also changed me on the inside, making me a stronger, more resilient, more compassionate person. I relate to others, particularly those with disabilities, in a way I never could before. Losing parts of my vision, ironically, has helped me see more clearly than ever.

ABOUT
JANNA HOLCOMB

Janna is a senior enlisted leader in the Air National Guard and has served for over twenty years as a committed mentor, advisor, and inspiration to the leaders of tomorrow. As a civilian, Janna has a wide range of experience as a successful entrepreneur, administrator, and federal employee. She holds master's degrees in Human Relations and International Relations, and is a passionate lifelong learner. Janna speaks four languages and uses her love of travel to immerse herself in other places and cultures. She spends much of her free time having dance parties with her daughters and husband, and aspires someday soon to have a small family farm where her family can be surrounded by flowers and animals.

Laurie G. Curtis

CHAPTER

MY CHOICE

By Laurie G. Curtis

I have learned life is not always fair or kind.

My Pastor would often say, "If you never faced a challenge, keep on living!"

I chuckle now because I have found that wisdom to be true. Regardless of how nice or kind you are, life is going to happen to you. You can experience the highest highs or the deepest lows.

Life can show you the deepest struggles you have ever seen. Those struggles can weigh on you to a point you don't know whether you are coming or going. It makes you feel like a dark cloud is blocking your hopes, dreams, desires, or will. Life can put you in a position where you are existing instead of living.

The funny thing is you may have gotten to this place by happenstance. Your actions don't always bring you the difficult situations you face, it can be done so by the action of others. Nonetheless here you are, so what do you do next?

After processing what has occurred, a choice has to be made.

You can either avoid the situation or deal with it. It is so easy to get lost in the situation, but the key to dealing with it for me was to change my mindset. I have found by changing my mindset, my outlook on difficult situations changes. I don't have it all figured out; instead I lean on my faith. Regardless of what happens in this situation, I trust ALL things will work for my good. Landing here didn't happen overnight, seeds for this outlook were planted years ago.

My fondest memories of my childhood in New York were of my mother singing in the church choir. My brother, sister, and I sat in a pew at the front of the church under the watchful eye (if you know what I mean) of our mother. I didn't always understand the emotions of what I was witnessing at that age, however, I always felt a sense of peace when I was in church. There was something about the pageantry, the music, and the energy that was uplifting to me.

One of my favorite songs the choir sang was "We Have Come This Far by Faith" by Albert A. Goodson. The words of the song let me know that I could lean on and trust in the word of God. The song, and my encounter with God at such an early age, would provide me with peace in my dark times knowing that by Faith, God would never fail me. This was tested after giving birth to my daughter.

Married with a 4 year old son, my husband and I planned to have another child and it didn't take us long to conceive. We were excited because my husband would be able to witness the birth of our second child unlike our first child. You see, my husband was stationed overseas, so he was not able to share my pregnancy experience or be present for the birth of our son.

We were excited about the new addition to our family. I even recall my son drawing a picture of our family with what would be his sister in my belly. No gender reveal parties back in my day!! My pregnancy was unremarkable… no morning sickness or swollen feet. I was active, and my test results were good. Overall, I felt great! And if the truth be told, I loved being pregnant!

As my due date approached, my husband became increasingly protective of me, to the point of getting on my nerves if I'm being honest. Since he missed the birth of our son, it was so important to him to see the birth of our second child.

On February 14, my aunt came into town from New York for a visit. We were shopping at the Mall when my contractions started; however, I didn't say anything since the contractions weren't bad. We made our way home. We cooked dinner, I got my bag and the baby's bag, and announced I was having contractions and we should call the doctor. My contractions increased in intensity and would stop me in my tracks. The frequency of the contractions also picked up. I became concerned I had waited too long and I would have the baby at the house.

After speaking to the doctor, we headed to the hospital, but we ran into a problem… I could not get downstairs. I was having a contraction every time I took a step, and I had to stop until they passed.

My husband wanted to carry me downstairs, but I was eventually able to get to the car on my own. We made it to the hospital. I was immediately taken to my room, and my husband parked the car. The nurse instructed me to change into a hospital gown. As I was changing, our daughter made her debut while I was standing by the side of the hospital bed. I delivered (well—caught) her on my own.

I was nowhere near the call button, so all I could do was shout for the nurses. They finally came and helped me get in the bed. As they worked on me and my daughter, all I could hear when my husband entered the room was him exclaiming …"You've got to be kidding!"

My husband missing the delivery of our daughter was a disappointment; however, it was overshadowed by the birth of his sweet valentine!

The birth of our daughter was a wonderful addition to our little family.

Our son was enjoying being a big brother and my husband and I were so proud of our family. As the months progressed we would take our daughter to her pediatrician for her check-ups. After her first birthday, we became concerned because she wasn't hitting her developmental milestones.

Little did we know this was just the tip of the iceberg.

Our daughter was a year and a half when she had her first seizure. It was the middle of the night and it came out of nowhere. She showed no signs of any issues during the day and she wasn't sick.

We immediately called 911. The EMTs came and transported her to our local hospital.

The doctors asked questions and conducted several tests including an MRI. According to the doctors, the scan showed something on her brain, and they wanted to transfer her to a hospital in Baltimore for further evaluation. Fortunately, there was nothing notable on the scan.

Our daughter was released and we scheduled a follow-up appointment with a neurologist. The rest of the year was spent at doctor's visits, undergoing tests, and eventually the diagnosis of epilepsy (or seizure disorder).

But there was more to come. My daughter was later found to be on the autism spectrum.

As a parent you have dreams for your children. For my daughter, it was going to sporting events, college, career, a wedding, and grandchildren. After her epilepsy and her autism diagnosis, my focus shifted. Instead of my dreams for her, we became focused on getting her all the help she needed to thrive based on her abilities.

Lauren was the center of our attention, but we realized we couldn't lose sight of our son and what he needed. My daughter's diagnosis didn't just impact her, it impacted the entire family.

It's hard to put into words what this journey has been like. What comes to mind is sadness, fear, frustration, guilt, and helplessness. Sadness and guilt are probably the biggest emotions I carried earlier on in this journey. Sadness for things not turning out as I had hoped for my daughter. And guilt for our son having to adjust to such a big issue at such a young age; and eventually having to take on the responsibility after I am gone.

My daughter is now 24. She is funny. Her smile and laugh will light up the room. She gives the best hugs, she loves to go for walks at the lake near our house, she loves music, and she has a mean two step!

I have an amazing support system made up of family, friends, teachers, community leaders and support staff. I could not have made it through the tough times without their love and support. When things get hard, I am reminded that I have come this far by faith. My faith is what sustains me. I trust I will get through whatever I am facing; and that in the end, my children will be okay.

God has proven this to be true in every situation I've faced. I don't struggle with the WHY, I focus on what IS, and what I need to do to move through it!

When I shifted my mindset from what my expectations were for my daughter to what makes her happy, it was life changing, and it brought me peace. I stopped trying to get her to conform to what I thought she should do, instead I focused on what she enjoyed doing.

Years ago, at work, I was sharing my frustration with one of my teachers, that it was difficult finding a Christmas or birthday gift for my daughter. She shared with me that her son had a disability and that she and her husband don't purchase gifts for their son, instead they share experiences with him. Their son loved to hike, so they would take him on hiking trips. That was a huge revelation for me.

I realized I was trying to put my daughter in a box, and she didn't fit. Ever since, I have focused on giving her experiences in areas that bring her joy!

Shifting my mindset allowed me to experience a deeper sense of joy, laughter, and love! I never pictured myself dealing with the challenges I have faced while raising my daughter. But what it has shown me is that life is a series of joyful and painful experiences. I often say that any difficult situation I face is what it is. No more no less.

I would be lying if I told you that the journey with my daughter has been easy. I can't control or change what has happened or going to happen for that matter. What I can do is choose how I respond to it, face it head on and look for the lessons the experience is there to teach me.

This journey has taught me that I am more than a conqueror.

I am resilient.

My faith and love have and will continue to sustain me as I chose to celebrate the wins and not dwell on the pain of the losses.

<u>Acknowledgement</u>

I would like to express my deepest thanks to my children, Benjamin and Lauren. Your love and support mean everything to me. I am truly honored to be called your Mom.

ABOUT
LAURIE G. CURTIS

Laurie Curtis is a mother, friend, leader, speaker, coach, and an encourager. She is a quiet force who speaks out loud, in an effort to motivate, share wisdom and lessons learned, when life presents us with difficult moments.

After the death of her husband, and faced with raising her two children, her daughter with special needs, Laurie had a choice to make. She could either throw in the towel, or acknowledge the situation for what it was, and move forward. Laurie did what she has done all her life. With her family and faith at the forefront of her mind, she made the decision to focus on her children, and dealt with them one day at a time.

It is Laurie's hope that in sharing her story and the lessons learned; people will see that regardless of what life throws at you, you have the strength, fortitude, and ultimately the choice in how you deal with it!

Residing in Maryland, Laurie is currently working on her first book with the intention of continuing to share her message of strength, hope, and the power of shifting your mindset when faced with difficult times. The biggest lesson Laurie has learned is that *Life is not always fair. It's not personal, it is what it is!*

Lori Blatt

CHAPTER

DEFINING MOMENTS

By Lori Blatt

January 19, 2005.

I t was my birthday, and I was going home.

It was an emotional day. My progress was measurable.

I'd met wonderful people who inspired me daily and had pushed me to my limit. I'd done a lot of soul-searching and hard work over the last several weeks.

No, I wasn't leaving a motivational seminar or inspirational retreat.

Far from it.

Two months earlier, I had been stripped of my health, my freedom to move and do as I want —things that I had taken for granted my whole life.

Instead, I was sitting in a wheelchair, waiting to be discharged from the physical therapy facility that had been my home for the last six weeks. It's where I spent Christmas day with my physical therapist learning to dress myself. A simple task I used to do every day without thinking about it.

Getting dressed took me three hours that day. Three LONG hours.

"Stop thinking from a place of pain. Stop thinking from a place of what happened to you...
and start thinking from a place of who you were created to be."

- Bishop TD Jakes

We all know people who are going through extremely hard times: illness, death, divorce, addiction, isolation. Life's curve balls.

I remember mine vividly.

I lay in a hospital bed unable to feel any sensation from my sternum down. I couldn't move my legs. I lost 90% of my arm strength and hand dexterity. My breathing became increasingly labored. My chest muscles tightened around my rib cage and wouldn't respond to my brain's request to "Relax."

A well-respected neurologist stood at my bedside, in his crisp white doctor's coat, blue oxford shirt and grey dress pants. He had just completed a brief exam as I lay motionless.

"The good news, Lori, is you're young and your prognosis for a full recovery is remarkably high. The bad news is your condition is going to get worse before it gets better."

Guillain-Barré syndrome (GBS) took me from an on-the-run mom and new business owner to a virtual quadriplegic over the course of *five days*. What started as a sinus infection sent my antibodies into a tailspin, wreaking havoc on my nervous systems, to the point that nurses placed a ventilator beside my ICU bed in case I stopped breathing.

That illness turned my world – and my family's world – upside down.

It shook me to my core.

It left me feeling vulnerable and fearful. Not only in the moment, but for years to come.

I get it. Whatever 'curveball' you're dealing with right now will consume every waking moment, every part of your life. Does it feel like you have a sign hanging over your head broadcasting your fear/lack/trauma? And that's all people can see?

Hell, it's all YOU can see.

Fear and anxiety do their best to isolate you. This life event begins to envelop you, define you. It did me.

Although the Guillain-Barré ran its course over eight weeks, it took two years to regain my physical strength. It was my mental strength that took the longest to recover.

It wasn't until a mastermind retreat in 2016 that I finally realized the power this illness still held over me. As we worked on our story, our 'why', the facilitator had us write down all our major life events to look for the trigger that had put us in the room that day. At the top of my list… my illness.

"*Those events are defining moments*," he said, "*and give us our uniqueness.*"

The light bulb went on.

It doesn't define you. It's a defining moment.

The "a-ha" felt like the gasp when cold water hits your face. I had allowed that one event to become a Scarlet Letter.

But I was the only one who could see it.

After 12 years, I was still letting it define me.

And so, the shift began.

I got to work releasing the victim mindset that had taken up residency in my head and left me feeling like I was wearing a suit of armor 24/7.

There were key decisions that put me back on the path to regain my balance and sense of worth:

Self-care

I studied and became certified in Reiki—a Japanese form of energy healing developed in 1920. Science tells us everything is made of energy. The same goes for people. We have the ability to balance our energy and that of others. Reiki was not just a technique I learned, but a way back to health and confidence.

Reading

Not only reading but learning and applying what I read. The insights, the fresh perspectives, the challenges to my current way of thinking were (and continue to be) invaluable, like this next reclaiming-sanity insight.

Profit First

I have been self-employed since 2003, launching the first iteration of my brand and marketing business on April 1 (20 months before my health derailment). It took me 15 years to learn how to deal with the stress of cash flow and self-employment taxes. Relief came in the form of a book, *Profit First* by Mike Michalowicz. In short, by setting up five bank accounts: Income, Owners Compensation, Operating Expenses, Taxes and Profit – and following a percentage system for dividing every business deposit received, I forced myself to SAVE. More importantly I forced myself to KNOW exactly what I had to spend in each of those areas. GAME. CHANGER.

Get a Coach

We don't know what we don't know... or perhaps more accurately, we can't change what we can't see because we're SO DEEP in it. A coach changes that dynamic. They are a sounding board, resource, and confidant. I have had business coaches, mindset coaches, financial coaches, fitness coaches and my personal favorite, a spiritual coach. Some may feel it's a luxury they can't afford. To me, it's non-negotiable.

Ask For/Hire Help

As the daughter of a blue-color workaholic, hard work was engrained in my psyche. Hiring help was 'soft'. Hiring someone to do something you could do yourself was a waste of money. So, I kept working 12-hour days with occasional all-nighters ... until I drove my body to the brink.

"You can do anything. You can't do everything."

- Greg McKeown, Essentialism

Love Your Work

If you don't love what you do, for goodness sakes STOP! Please take note, I did not say "Do what you love," but rather love the work you're doing RIGHT NOW. A wonderfully wise lesson pulled from my reading of *Time Warrior* by Steve Chandler. This decision alone can shift your mindset 180 degrees. Love what you do while working on a plan to make a living doing what you love.

This curveball you were thrown, yes, it sucks. It's not fair and it's okay to be angry. But IT IS LIFE and as overwhelming as it feels right now, it's just part of your bigger journey. This event alone does not define you. What defines you is the mindset you choose and the actions you take despite the pain, tears, struggle, depression and the unknown.

The worst events can be life-transforming gifts — IF we look beyond the initial shock, pain, and disruption.

So, this isn't a story about illness. My illness was a merely the catalyst needed to cause a shift and teach me two lessons:

Lesson #1 was to stop burning the candle at both ends like it was a badge of honor. It literally made me sick. I believe with my whole being that my earth-shaking illness was the Universe's way of getting my attention and showing me that I was working ridiculously hard, but not very smart.

Lesson #2 was a chance to really understand what it takes to BE well. Not *just* physically, but financially, relationally, emotionally, and spiritually, too.

This turned out to be a story about my awakening.

"Step out of your past and into your destiny." - Bishop TD Jakes

I swore to myself I would never feel that helpless and be paralyzed, literally or figuratively, ever again. The insecurities that my illness unleashed had held me back for years.

Today it is the fuel that gets me up every morning grateful and a better person for having lived it.

So, whatever you're facing right now, sit with it, stare at it, acknowledge it, then release it. It will only define you if you allow it. Instead, see this as a defining moment and an opportunity to realign your priorities and sense of self, to take inventory and BE intentional with your thoughts, words, and actions.

If you're in a tough place right now, the good news is it's temporary.

The even better news is YOU decide what now, what next?

BE well.

- L

ABOUT
LORI BLATT

Lori Blatt is a creative soul living in an analytical mind, resulting in a holistic balance of marketing principles, provocative questions, engaging design and well-crafted words. She has the ability to see the BIG picture and the design prowess to execute the details. Lori loves using these gifts to help clients weave their passion and energy into their personal brand, so they feel connected with what makes them unique and stand out in a noisy world.

She is a mom of three boys, wife, dog lover, brand builder, marketing maven, Medium.com writer, Reiki Practitioner, tiny house enthusiast, VRBO host, margarita connoisseur, and old soul (the order varies daily).

www.blattcom.net
www.the-meraki-blueprint.com
https://www.linkedin.com/in/loriblatt/
https://medium.com/@LoriBlatt

Steph Annie Cutler

CHAPTER

FIRST STEPS
OF FREEDOM

By Steph Annie Cutler

My freedom was the best gift I ever received from my ex. Most people chuckle hearing this. Although the reaction initially struck me as odd, I now understand it.

For those who haven't experienced a deeply abusive relationship lacking knowledge of personal autonomy and confidence in voice to choose to leave, it is abnormal and therefore takes a moment to comprehend.

We had spoken of babies and moving in together. In my mind we had been building a life with one another.

The moment we said goodbye, I was sitting in a garage turned game room connected to a house full of people celebrating my adopted grandma's birthday, on a perfectly blissful Autumn evening in Arizona. Phone pressed firmly to my ear while tears streamed down my face, contacts cloudy. My head was swimming and I refused to hide my crying. I didn't nor couldn't attempt to speak to anybody.

The night drew along. The party passed.

The next morning, while waiting to fly home I texted him. I asked, "Why can't you go to therapy, and we work things out?"

I wish I could say I didn't ask him to work on things.

For his breakup speech he acknowledged his complete lack of empathy for me. Yes, he did the whole, "It's not you, it's me," followed by innocuous statements regarding his friend providing him this insight.

He lacked empathy for me, in totality.

I don't remember his response verbatim, but THANK GOD for the unequivocal no.

I cried… for days.

I was deeply wounded from this perceived rejection.

I needed to let go of everything.

He was embedded in my everyday routine.

I had to rebuild. Start anew.

I'd like to say it was easy since our year long relationship had been long-distance the entire time, but after spending everyday connecting.

His absence was stifling.

I was fortunate to have been rooming with *my person* and their husband at the time.

My person, they're the only person who was truly there for me in my young adult life to lean on, open up to, to be authentically me especially when I didn't yet know who I really was. She did; from moment one she was safe, loving, kind, and always honest and supportive.

The two of them, my person and her husband, true to form, provided a safe and supportive space for me to process, feel, be seen and vent without judgment.

So much of my time had been consumed by my previous companion, now ex. This time and space I now had provided clarity to all that our previous relationship actually was.

I began to heal.

My healing certainly did not happen overnight.

It was a choice I made after being set free from the all-encompassing toxic and abusive relationship. Every single day it was a choice I made. A commitment to become more than I had previously allowed myself to be.

I chose to sit with myself.

I chose to learn and understand myself.

I chose to identify my needs.

I chose to change the ways in which I showed up that were toxic, unhealthy, and born of the deep wounds inflicted by childhood trauma, as well as the ones endured from my ex.

I had been carrying such finely ingrained baggage during the relationship I failed to trust the red and yellow flags as I had seen them. My memory began repressing moments in our shared experiences and my voice officially hid in a dark abyss, rendering it absent. My presence had become so fragmented, I no longer recognized myself.

I refused to stay, sitting in my own way.

I chose to find how to reclaim my power.

I made a commitment to never be treated in such abusive ways again at the permission of my fearfully silent submission.

I had to change. I didn't want to be who I had been in *that* relationship (or the past 27 years of my life), ever again. With the loving support of my person and their husband in a safe, stable environment I did the work to heal and evolve.

I inhabited my room in silence, often crying, immensely uncomfortable allowing my emotions, memories, thoughts, beliefs, and understandings to surface organically. I identified the egregious violations I endured. I transitioned into taking responsibility for my emotionally and verbally volatile behavior. Then, as I developed a feeling of safety inside my own body, I worked on forgiving myself and changing the way I showed up for ME.

When it would become too much, or I needed a break from processing I used my phone to distract and divert my processing energy to whatever tv show I had on. When I began fast-forwarding through 90% of a show, it was time to switch to reading. My reading consisted of books purchased throughout previous years, such as *NonViolent Communication* by Marshall Rosenberg, Ph.D. I also read *Getting the Love That You Want* by Harville Hendrix and the *Dance of Anger* by Harriet Lerner.

It was the divinely orchestrated introduction to a Homeostatic Restorative therapist who provided the insight and guidance to create a feeling of safety within my own body, so I could responsibly live here. This supportive guidance accelerated my understanding and therefore my healing.

Note: For individuals who have endured trauma it can be common to stay in our head which means behaving in pure survival mode: fight, flight, freeze or appease (reactivity). We don't yet know how to emotionally regulate because being fully in our bodies and choosing to cognitively respond to our experience is required. Homeostatic Restorative therapy builds a foundation to shift from reactive to responsive through breathwork and guided meditations.

Homeostatic Restorative therapy taught me how to emotionally regulate through living in my body, connecting with my breath, identifying how I feel and what I need. It developed my self-awareness, voice, and confidence. It also expanded my sliver of personal autonomy. I was learning myself from my soul while developing a relationship with God/Source. I was intentionally healing physically, mentally, and emotionally.

Naturally, this endeavor unearthed painful and heart-churning memories, uncomfortable false beliefs, past regrets, cringe-worthy moments for me. Being willing to look at who I had become was inarguably necessary and the result was something far greater than I could have begun to fathom.

In freedom, I chose to put forth the effort. I was reclaiming my power. Willingly looking with clear eyes at all parts of me and experiences from my past. As repressed memories surfaced, I acknowledged their truth before transmuting them. I acknowledged, forgave, and released myself from such harsh experiences and spiteful words. I refused their attachment to my soul's identity.

I genuinely wish those who violated me consciousness, healing, and authentic love.

Even more, I took responsibility for my past behaviors, words, and beliefs. I forgave myself of all I did and said that harmed others and myself.

I started a path leading me to divine neutrality. Neutralizing deep and immense pain, identifying false beliefs, and conditioning and releasing all things as they no longer serve my highest good.

I now choose to remain introspective and confident in who I am, making intentional progress towards my dreams, which fulfills me. I am living a life that is safe, loving, joyful, playful, and successful in all the ways I desire. It has taken great effort and time, and with it I have arrived.

In my freedom, having chosen to walk the path which demanded I traverse the vast profound I met myself there and reclaimed all of me.

For those of you reading this, it's possible for you too. I invite you to identify what opportunities you have to create freedom in your life. This is your invitation to reflect on your own experience and see the potential in creating the everyday moments of freedom and self-love that you've been craving.

What experiences and events in your past give insight into what you will and won't allow?

Are you being who you want to be? If not, what can you shift or release to take a step closer to becoming that person who lives freely?

What resources, people, books, podcasts, do you have access to that you might not have considered that can support you in your efforts?

It takes conscious effort to walk the path of learning who you are and unlearning everything else.

I can attest that the effort required is worth it.

ABOUT
STEPH ANNIE CUTLER

Steph Annie Cutler is an advocate and facilitator of the trauma-informed approach to healing. As Founder of Insightful Annie, she has combined her personal experience with continuing education to support others to achieve a life that is built on a deep sense of self, love, joy, and safety. A published author and frequent speaker on the topics such as mental health, recovery from abuse, personal responsibility, effective communication and inclusivity, Steph Annie strives to reshape the status quo for relationships. She strongly believes that when we each take accountability for ourselves and our own healing, we begin to create space and invite others to do the same. She loves to hold space and provide reflections to individuals who are ready to question the foundation of their identity and release their past experiences to become who they've always desired to be.

Leslie Grodin

CHAPTER

THE GIFT OF STORY: A JOUNREY BACK TO SELF

By Leslie Grodin

ave you ever noticed people being ugly to one another, through words or actions? When I began to notice this in myself, it left me not liking who I was being. This awareness forced me to take a deep introspective look at myself and my mindset. In doing so, I become more aware that my initial reactions/thoughts about a person I encountered were not always positive. Who am I to judge anyone? In that moment, I made a conscious choice to be kinder to others, starting with the thoughts in my own mind.

What better time than the beginning of a new year! I started making New Year's resolutions that would support me in being a better ME to others. New Year's resolution #1 was to **correct negative first instinctual thought**s. This change was no easy task if I'm honest.

First, you have to acknowledge you do it. Then you have to be aware enough in the moment to ask yourself, "How do you know this is true?" When the answer is, "you don't know that it's true" then you must be willing to replace the negative thought with something positive.

The following year, I introduced a second New Year's resolution. I made the resolution to **smile at everyone I walked by**. Smiling became a habit, something I still do, automatically, years later, without any effort. Throughout the pandemic I found myself doing it underneath my mask. I know I could feel that energy and I like to believe the people I was smiling at could see the kindness in my eyes.

I have always been curious about people's stories. For example, a few times a week, I would see a certain woman leaving my neighborhood. She was thin, had a pixie cut, always well dressed, with a Starbucks drink in hand, and pulling a suitcase behind her. One day, unlike the other days, I saw her close up for the first time. Her weathered face and hands led me to assume she was homeless.

I was curious to learn more about her, I found myself wanting to ask her one day if I could buy her that cup of coffee from Starbucks. I would invite her to sit down and talk, and I would listen to her story. Would she be open to that? Or would that offend her? Would she be nice?

I will never know... I never saw her again. I never got to ask the million questions swirling around in my mind. I'm not sure if it was part of the natural progression of life, the "older and wiser" theory, or subconsciously I desired to be seen and heard.

I didn't want the opportunity to ask someone a question about themselves slip through my fingers again. I had the idea to start a YouTube channel where I would interview people and share their stories. In the fall of 2019, I filmed my first episode of *I Want To Know Your Story*. I would go on to film and post over 100 interviews on YouTube. I had the opportunity to meet some incredible people, a few who are a part of this book project.

It was amazing that going up to someone and asking them if they wanted to sit down for a conversation typically led to a YES! I would meet people in parking lots, on social media, and of course referrals from those who did their own interviews. I met people who started nonprofits, produced major television shows, and had major life events they wanted to share. They were all willing to open up and share their story with me. In turn, allowing me to share it with others. I was so humbled by these conversations and this experience. It truly was a gift to be able to film these interviews over two years and pivot to doing them online instead of in person during COVID.

Part of the motivation to do these interviews was the comments from those I was interviewing about how happy they were to have shared their story. The biggest compliments that I got were how others felt about being given the opportunity to share, and how present I was with them during our conversation. I made it a point to never prepare my questions ahead of time (except for the core 3 that are in every interview). I wanted people watching to get to know them, just as I did. It was my hope that people would realize that you really don't know that person that you were walking by, passing judgment on. They just might surprise you.

My life was enriched by those that I interviewed, a lot of whom I still communicate with to this day. My gratitude to them is unexplainable. I was going through a very tough time and each and every person showed me that there was power in positivity, humanity, and sharing yourself with others.

In August 2019, I took a trip to Europe, specifically Greece, Croatia, Montenegro, and Venice. In each location, I booked a tour guided by locals. Each local guide was kind and eager to share information about their hometown and their lives. In a way, this was their way of sharing their stories with me. A few of the tour guides I met were around the same age as me. It was awesome to see how happy everyone was, and so proud to share more about their culture. The energy in each of these places was so different from what I experienced here in the US.

It was nearly the 21st century and in these countries, life was observably different. I couldn't flush my toilet paper, a convenience I'm accustomed to. The houses were older and often smaller, several generations under one roof, and the people were noticeably HAPPY. It forced me to look at things from a different perspective. Was I focusing on the wrong things, was I looking at "things" to make me happy? The answer was yes, I was. I arrived at the knowing that happiness comes from within and is a conscious choice. At that moment, I reminded myself that I too chose to be happy.

Upon returning from my trip, I started meditating daily. Then, in October of 2019, I took a yoga class with a friend. I had taken yoga classes before and wasn't a fan. However, this time it was going to be different. I was more open to the mental aspects of the class and powered through the physical part of the class.

I was hooked and wanted to sign up for the free week of classes. I went every day and was committed to taking full advantage of the free classes. After a short delay, I was sidelined for an injury that required surgery, I finally was able to sign up at the studio and began attending class two times a week. The course was taught by an instructor who always seemed to theme his class to where I was that day.

Two months later… the world shut down. I didn't let that discourage me, I was still meditating every day, sometimes twice a day, morning and evening. I started taking the yoga classes via an online app offered by the studio as their way of continued classes during the pandemic.

One year after starting to take classes, I enrolled in my first Teacher Training. Shortly after, I enrolled in another teacher training and then one more following that. I am now certified to teach three styles of yoga. Yoga Sculpt, Hot Power Fusion, and Yoga Nidra. I love the variety - each offering something unique.

Sculpt is high energy- giving students the option to use weights

Hot Power Fusion is a set sequence of postures

Yoga Nidra is purely meditative - done in comfort and stillness

As someone who has experienced anxiety most of my life and been a little tightly wound, yoga has given me the tools to access what is within me to manage my anxiety in a new and healthier way. Friends that have known me for years were completely shocked that I now teach and take so many yoga classes.

As someone who also suffered from a diagnosis of Ulcerative Colitis since my early 20s. I found my symptoms to be triggered mostly by stress and anxiety. 2020, the year that was the hardest for most of us, was the first year since age 25 that I did not have to have a colonoscopy due to being symptomatic.

I truly feel that the shift in my mindset and allowing myself to let go of a lot of mental tension have led me to feel so much better. I still have minor flare-ups, but nothing like before and easily controlled and remedied.

The work I have put in over the last four years allowed me the strength and the proper mindset to step away from a life that was no longer serving me. The changes allowed me to believe in myself, to know what I deserve, to allow me to love myself more, and find the inner strength to walk away.

This introspective look at my life took me on a journey to become a better human, not only for myself, but for others. I thank you for reading my story, my journey, and allowing me to share this part of myself with you. Holding space for yourself is so important and I encourage you to give yourself the time and space you deserve.

I invite you to contact me to start your own journey. I would be honored to guide you in a meditation or a yoga practice in one of the styles that I mentioned above.

ABOUT
LESLIE GRODIN

Leslie Grodin was born in Las Vegas, Nevada. Growing up she moved around a lot, going to 9 schools in 12 years, in three different states on two different sides of the country. She finally moved back to California, where she had spent her freshman year of high school, to complete her senior year. She would then go off to college at UCSB, yet another move. After college she would remain in Santa Barbara for an additional 16 years. Part of that was being able to create the stability that she was never in control of throughout her childhood. Five and a half years after graduating college she started her long-time career in medical sales. She enjoyed sales, but more importantly she was able to help doctors help people. Leslie has always been a "people person" curious about their stories and motivations.

Throughout her early forties she would embark on a journey or personal growth and connection. She hopes you enjoy hearing about that in the chapter she contributed to this book.

Carly J. Bressler-Archambeau

CHAPTER

FINDING MY WAY THROUGH UNEXPECTED CAREGIVING

By Carly J. Bressler-Archambeau

In July 2021, my husband received a call that his mother — who had type two diabetes and a lengthy list of comorbidities — was hospitalized due to blood sugar control issues. The month before she spent several days in the hospital for a similar issue.

My husband's uncle urged him to come home because there was more going on than a couple of blood sugar management hiccups. My husband made the trip from North Carolina to New Hampshire that same day.

Upon arrival, my husband debriefed with more of his family and the medical team at the hospital.

The two hospital stays in short succession showed us that there were new challenges in independently managing her diabetes. But what caused this change? For the entire duration of my experience with her, my mother-in-law had type two diabetes and managed it independently.

Like many aging adults, she was certainly not well off financially, but she was self-sufficient, making the drive from her shared house in New Hampshire to her family in Massachusetts at least a few times a year. She managed her own medical care, including many doctors' appointments and medications, handled her own finances, did her own grocery shopping and her own cleaning.

At the hospital, my husband learned from the medical team that the forgetfulness we had witnessed sometimes was no longer akin to the common memory issues we all tend to face with aging. Instead, my mother-in-law's condition could now be diagnosed as dementia. With the progression, her seemingly dramatic challenges in managing her diabetes made sense. The doctors shared with us that with her state she likely forgot to eat or to give herself the correct insulin dosage before a meal.

Somewhere since our prior visit, she had also been upgraded from oral medications to manage her diabetes to sliding-scale insulin. A sliding-scale insulin protocol requires the patient to check their blood sugar before a meal and to administer a dose of insulin from a pen. The insulin dose corresponds to the blood sugar reading and must be carefully selected and administered. Accidentally giving oneself too much insulin can result in dangerously low blood sugars whereas giving oneself too little can result in dangerously high blood sugar. Unfortunately, sliding-scale insulin and dementia are a dangerous combination.

We surmised given the progression of her memory loss and the complexities of managing sliding-scale insulin as part of her diabetes management, the two recent hospitalizations would be commonplace without intervention. The medical team agreed and recommended my mother-in-law have help at home – perhaps from her housemate – to manage the insulin or relocate somewhere with greater assistance.

While my mother-in-law's housemate was eager to help in any way she could, we agreed that my mother-in-law should be with family. My husband recently retired from the military and was not working. So, we rapidly made the arrangements to move my mother-in-law from her long-time home in New Hampshire to our home in North Carolina. Within just 24 hours, flights were arranged, short-term prescriptions to bridge the gap from discharge to establishing care with a new primary care provider were arranged, new health insurance coverage was lined up, and her new room was prepared.

The first few days after her arrival were pleasant. We all tried to get into our new routine, my husband and I learning all of the medications, the sliding scale insulin, the foods that were tolerated well and those that were not. By the fourth day, my mother-in-law started asking how long she was "visiting" and when she would "go home," sometimes packing up her suitcase, ready for the departure that would happen. Those conversations between my husband and his mom were heartbreaking – reinforcing the reality that she was living with us for good because she could not safely care for herself had to be shared. Sometimes she was mad, other times she was sad. She often shared that she wanted her car back so she could at least drive herself around and learn her new surroundings.

Alas, the doctors had agreed she should not be allowed to drive – her memory issues and lagging reflexes and response time due to many years of coping with a back injury and neuropathy made driving an unsafe option. This transition – including the repeated discussions about these big life changes – wore on my husband. His mom may not remember the discussions that had been had; he remembered each and every one.

Over the course of our relationship before this abrupt change to all of our lives, my mother-in-law and I were not close. While fortunate that she was not the "monster-in-law" sometimes joked about, our generational differences, our backgrounds and experiences, and our general attitudes and worldviews were markedly different. Over the years, we had managed being pleasant enough during lengthy visits and family trips, but the new permanency of our multigenerational household challenged us both.

Little things got to me in those early days – my favorite Lilo and Stitch pajamas had accidentally been left in a drawer in the room that became hers; she was so tickled when she found these cute pajamas that she had forgotten about buying, I didn't have the heart to reclaim them. She would sneak food to her room – usually a special chocolate or treat I had tucked away for me. She was often belligerent and nasty to my husband – especially about her desire to have her car and to drive or about not having some of her certain (not-diabetic friendly!) food in the house. Under normal circumstances, I would have confronted her, perhaps even asked her to head back to New Hampshire. But our home was now her home. And, I had to remind myself daily, she was not the same person anymore. Dementia was chipping away not *just* at her memory but also at her personality and behaviors.

We quickly learned a key part of her struggles with managing her diabetes were food preferences, not only the memory issues impeding her ability to manage the various diabetes medications and blood sugar checks. We found her eating spoonfuls of jelly from the jar. Another time, she took scoops of stevia from the container we kept by the coffee pot. If left unsupervised, she would snack endlessly and typically on foods that were not the best choice for a diabetic.

We made adjustments to what food we kept on hand and what was readily available. We placed a childproof lock on the pantry door. We relocated certain food from the fridge in the kitchen to the fridge in the garage, carefully hiding things like applesauce and jelly to deter her from gorging. We kept fresh fruits and vegetables with a lower glycemic index available to her – like berries and grape tomatoes to quell her sweet tooth. We invested in low carb snack bars, left on the counter with nuts and other snack items. Eventually we got into a groove with our caregiving routine, finding go-to foods that she liked and that did not spike her blood sugar.

As we worked through this transition into full-time caregiving and trying to meet her needs, life also continued on. I was just a few months into a new job and going to school for a doctorate. Our five year old son started kindergarten and soccer. My husband continued to look for work in his field with hopes of starting his second career.

In November 2021, my husband received a fabulous job offer – a position in civilian service, working for the federal government, in his military specialty. The offer, however, meant relocation. We took the chance and moved to South Carolina.

By the end of December 2021, we moved into our new home and started this new chapter in our life. My husband started his new job, my son started at his new school, and I built a new routine, juggling my remote workload while now being the primary caregiver for my mother-in-law during the weekdays. Unfortunately, the massive amount of change that often comes with a move – the inconsistencies in my exercise regularity, irregularities in healthy eating, disruptions to sleep and rest, constant unpacking and rearranging, and lack of social support – took a toll.

I was cranky, bitter, and resentful about the situation. While I loved working from home, I had a growing dislike of having to work my day around meals and medications. I blamed my mother-in-law. The rational part of my brain reasoned that her condition was not her fault, but the chimp side of my brain was pissy.

My inner monologue was in a vicious cycle – frustration and annoyance towards my mother-in-law why she allowed this situation to happen – "Why didn't she take better care of herself? Why isn't there more money to cover all of this stuff? Why does she have to be here?" The rational side of my brain would then counter – "You know this isn't her fault. She didn't choose to have diabetes or dementia. She didn't choose to

THE WHAT NOW MINDSET

have no other option than to live with you. She doesn't even want to be here but has nowhere else she can live safely. Stop being so childish and selfish." And on and on it went.

I was in a dangerous spiral of negativity. Something had to give otherwise I feared I would implode!

So, what now?

I cut back on alcohol. Wine was so easy to turn to in the evenings when I was burnt out and frustrated, and yet set me up for an even fouler mood the next day. Rather than going cold turkey, I focused on mindfulness. I downloaded an app on my phone to help me track how much I was drinking. I set goals each week to have a little less. I started sleeping and feeling better.

I focused on doing the things I love – I started running and reading again. I woke earlier than before if I wanted to get a run in before my husband went to work, or I adjusted my work schedule to get a run in during the few hours three days a week that a paid caregiver was at the house to help my mother-in-law. I needed to get out of the house a bit on the weekends – whether that be a long run or going to the library or a kid's event with our son. I started to end each day with reading a few pages before bed, instead of sitting in front of the TV with a glass of wine.

My husband and I worked to be more open and honest in our communication, including sharing our needs and wants. We found a capable babysitter for our son who was also comfortable working with an aging person with dementia and reinstituted date nights. We even found that a casual "at-home" date night – a charcuterie board and a game of chess – could work wonders for our relationship and morale.

I started therapy – as uncomfortable as it can be to be honest with ourselves, let alone sharing our innermost thoughts with another. I needed an objective perspective to tame the circular, self-defeating thought patterns I had developed as part of caring for my mother-in-law. It is amazing what good therapy can do to help reset perspective!

At the time of this writing, we are now nine months into our caregiving journey, four of those months in our new home. Some days, I just have to focus on doing the things that need done, with low expectations: check the blood sugar, give the medicine, make the meal, check on the trash and the laundry, make small talk and be pleasant.

Other days, it is nice to talk to my mother-in-law, to watch a movie as a family or play a game of Cribbage. This season is a difficult one – any of us sandwich generation caregivers who are juggling caring for kids and aging parents have many challenges to work through. I also know this season will not be forever. So, I am going to continue to fake it until I make it on the days that are tough and embrace and savor the little wonderful moments.

ABOUT
CARLY J. BRESSLER-ARCHAMBEAU

With a love for serving others, **Carly** is an experienced healthcare professional who has worked the continuum of care – from the hospital bedside caring for patients as a physical therapist assistant to developing and orchestrating complex strategic plans for quality and program improvement in managed care. A passion for learning and growth, Carly is currently working towards a Ph.D. in Health Services, with a concentration in Leadership, and holds degrees in Master of Public Health and Bachelor of Science in Public Health.

Carly lives in the Greater Charleston area (South Carolina) area with her husband, five-year old son, mother-in-law, beagle, and black cat. Future additions to the family will include another dog and lots of fish! In addition to her passion for her family (both human and of the furry variety), Carly enjoys reading Enola Holmes mysteries and sports psychology books, exploring new trails on foot at home and afar, and trying new recipes (while minimizing undercooking poultry!).

Carly firmly believes that with coffee and wine, all things are possible!

Xavier Whitford

CHAPTER

PAIN INTO PURPOSE

By Xavier Whitford

I used to say that my life was a series of unfortunate events; from being sexually abused as a child to being raped at the age of fourteen. This was followed by a series of terrible and unhealthy decisions made from a wounded and broken young girl. I found myself married and pregnant at the age of nineteen.

The day my beautiful boy, Tommy, was born was the happiest day of my life.

I had always dreamed of being a mother and the moment I saw his sweet face, I fell instantly in love. God had given me the greatest gift and I wasn't about to take it for granted or allow the sins of my past to tarnish his future.

What now?

There I was, a nineteen-year-old mom, in an abusive marriage, committed to building a better life for me and Tommy. Then my husband died. My son was 3 years old, and I was pregnant with my daughter.

What now?

I knew I had to fight hard to provide a better future for my children. I focused on going to college while working a full-time job and being the best mother I could be. I thought that would be the worst thing I would experience in my life, but it wasn't.

I finished college and provided a decent life for my kids, but it wasn't easy. Eventually, I fell in love with a wonderful man, and we married six years after the loss of my first husband.

However, we had our ups and downs as all families do.

My son struggled mentally and emotionally his whole life over the loss of his father. He struggled with accepting another man in life as a dad. To most people he showed a smiling, funny, loving, and talented young man. Those closest to him saw the anger, pain, and sadness he struggled through.

We did everything we could to help and support him through it all. Many visits to counselors, doctors, therapists, and rehabs. There was nothing I wouldn't have done to help my son.

Many moments in my life I had to stop and ask myself:

What now?

However, the most defining moment was in August of 2014 when I found my son Tommy after he had taken his life by suicide.

What do you do when you find your first born and only son dead? I remember thinking there is no way I can survive this. I remember questioning, "Why me."

I remember considering giving up all together myself. Ultimately, I decided there had to be a purpose in my pain.

I choose to trust that God would make this horrible and painful experience into something good. I made the decision not to be silent about Tommy's death or the struggle he fought each and every day.

I decided my story wasn't over and neither was Tommy's.

I wanted to be an example to others, someone who could stand strong on their faith foundation. Someone who could not just survive but thrive despite the pain and grief. I knew Tommy would want that as well.

I wanted my daughter and granddaughter to look at me and know that they were loved and supported, and that we would get through this. I wanted to trust God and believe that this pain would lead me to a greater destiny.

It has been my experience that with pain comes fear. I didn't want the fear or pain to control my life, the life of my family, or our future. To be honest, I was consumed by fear after losing Tommy because if this could happen to him, it could happen to anyone. In the past, my pain would have stopped me from acting, however, this time I used my pain and fear as a catapult to act.

I used pain's energy to take action and make an ignited change. Through every step and each opportunity, I honored Tommy. I was terrified of judgment. I was terrified of failing. Talking about my personal story of great loss, pain, and uninformed decisions puts me in a very vulnerable spot. Helping others by creating support groups puts me in an emotional spot. But all of that is not worse than sitting back and doing nothing out of fear of giving into my pain. So, I did it.

I started a blog nineteen days after losing Tommy, *Each Breath of Faith*. I refused to let my son's death be for nothing. I wanted a way to share our journey and educate others. I knew the only way I could continue without my boy was to fight for and honor him every day, just as I did when he was alive.

The fight against suicide helps me heal and gives me a purpose through the pain I endure daily. My hope has always been that through sharing our story I would encourage, inspire, and help others. I have witnessed how sharing your story unlocks the door to others sharing theirs. I now understand that through sharing, real healing and change happen.

I have met many people who have shared their stories and helped me better understand what my son was going through in his pain.

I have been encouraged and inspired by so many suicide survivors that choose to live and use their pain to help others.

My own journey through depression, anxiety, and crippling PTSD because of finding Tommy that day, has allowed me to better understand what others go through. Fighting through my own mental health challenges has equipped me to be more compassionate, empathetic, and understanding.

We established the Tommy Corral Memorial Foundation (TCMF) to provide needed mental health and suicide prevention training in churches, schools, and business organizations across the world. We have been so fortunate to even share our story in Sweden and Japan, thanks to the virtual world we live in. Establishing mental health support groups for teens, young adults, and grieving mothers provides a safe place to share their feelings and connect with others who struggle in similar ways.

We provide financial support to individuals needing counseling, therapy, or medication who do not have insurance or financial means to pay for the needed treatment. This allows us to fulfill a need we saw in our community. This financial support has allowed hundreds of individuals to receive hope and healing they needed to get them through a dark time.

TCMF offers workshops and retreats focused on improving our mental health and building resiliency through Yoga, Meditation, Reiki, and Art. We offer opportunities for individuals to connect with their feelings and restore their mental health by learning positive coping strategies.

The retreats have offered a beautiful and safe place for people to focus on where they are, where they want to be and build skills to get there.

Through the years, we have grown beyond what we ever thought possible, but at the heart of it all is our love and honor of the person Tommy was and the life he led. TCMF works to reduce the stigma and bring hope and healing to others, so they don't have to fight alone. I genuinely believe that finding a purpose in my pain was the answer to my what now question after losing my son.

Never would I have imagined my life or purpose being working to support individuals living with mental illness and experiencing suicidal thoughts. God has equipped me with the strength and words to help in ways I could never have done myself.

Each day that goes by, I learn so much more and although we may never know the impact we have made. I pray that we have made Tommy proud and saved some lives.

My encouragement to you is when you find yourself at a crossroad where you are asking yourself what now; believe that with wounds comes wisdom and with pain comes purpose.

You are stronger than you know and will get through whatever it is you're going through.

You are not alone.

Use that pain to catapult you into the greatest purpose of your life and find your own—

What now?

Acknowledgments and Dedication

I would like to extend my heartfelt gratitude to my husband, Cory, and daughter, Makaya, for always supporting me in following my purpose and sharing our story in hopes to inspire and encourage others. I also want to especially thank Crystal & Anne for being a part of establishing TCMF from the very beginning and who still fight alongside me to this very day. Thank you to our dear friends Jan and Wynford for your continued support and encouragement daily. Thank you to our past and current board members, donors, and volunteers who help make all we do possible.

I am eternally grateful and thankful for the love and mercy of Jesus Christ and the purpose and strength He has instilled in me through this journey.

I dedicate this chapter to my beautiful son, Tommy, and every person who has shared their story with me or that we have been able to help in some way. I see you. I thank you. You are enough. You are brave. You are loved.

Everything I do is to honor God and my precious boy, Tommy, who I miss dearly every minute of every day. I love you Tommy and I hope that I have made you proud. Your bright smile and personality are missed immensely.

ABOUT
XAVIER WHITFORD

Xavier Whitford is the Founder and Executive Director of the Tommy Corral Memorial Foundation. She has devoted her life to helping others who live with mental illness or been affected by suicide loss. After losing her son Tommy to suicide and experiencing her own challenges through anxiety, depression, and post-traumatic stress disorder, Xavier found a deep purpose in her pain to help others.

Xavier shares her story to help others find courage and strength to rise above the pain, stigma, and shame of mental illness. Xavier is a Board Member, Speaker, and Trainer with the National Alliance on Mental Illness, Northern Illinois chapter. She is also a certified Mental Health First Aid Instructor and Group Facilitator. She is a contributing author of the book "It's Ok to Not Be Ok" and a survivor.

She is a frequent speaker at schools, churches, and organizations inspiring and educating groups of all ages to end the stigma surrounding mental illness and on the factors that lead to suicide. Xavier helps arm individuals within communities with support and training. Her personal story, tireless commitment, and passion to improve support and education around these topics has made her a powerful advocate to the mental health community.

Her greatest joy is the time she spends with her husband, daughter, and granddaughter.

Follow Xavier on Facebook and Instagram or contact her at

TCMF21@gmail.com

www.tommycorralmemorialfoundation.com

https://www.facebook.com/eachbreathoffaith/

https://www.facebook.com/xavierwhitford

Instagram: @TCMF21

Kristin Murner

CHAPTER

DON'T WORSHIP
THE THORN

By Kristin Murner

E arly one spring morning, I stood at the top of my stairs calling for my seven year-old son.

Where was he?!

Panic was slowly rising through my body and my voice was increasing in volume as I called for him. His bed was empty. He was nowhere to be found.

I checked the alarm panel, but no one had opened the doors.

Where was he?!

I raced through the perimeter of every room and couldn't find Eli.

Back at the bottom of the stairs I heard a little, sleepy voice, "Mom, why was I sleeping in Lydia's closet?"

Several months prior, Eli said he was having trouble seeing the board at school. All of us wear glasses, and I assumed he was nearsighted like his sister. I made an appointment with our family optometrist and didn't think much of it. That all changed when the doctor displayed a single, massive capital "R" on the screen.

"Lower case "N." Eli confidently declared.

I knew immediately something was very, very wrong. As the exam went on, it became clear we were dealing with something serious, rare, and likely genetic. Whatever it was warranted a referral to Boston's Mass Eye and Ear hospital, where world-renowned specialists could make a clear diagnosis.

Don't Worship the Thorn

While we waited the long six weeks for the referral, I spent too much time researching. I was a regional sales rep at a large educational company working in nurse education. I was surrounded by compassionate medical professionals who were both friends and colleagues, and none of them knew much about the most likely diagnoses in front of us. The conditions were all incurable. One was neurological, and fatal within a handful of years. I stopped searching and on one overwhelming Saturday afternoon, took a long shower, and wept.

I also surrendered it all back to God.

We are a family of strong faith. I could lay down the fear and need to control things, I just wasn't ready to give back my son.

In the Bible, the Apostle Paul repeatedly asked God to take away a 'thorn in his side.'

God reminds Paul that His grace is sufficient to bear it (2 Corinthians 12:9), and as I sat with what I knew was a diagnosis that would forever change our family, I didn't want to worship our "thorn"–whatever it was– but the One who would carry us through.

Bolstered by the prayers of our church family and support of my colleagues, friends and family, my husband and I left the girls with dear friends and trekked the 150 miles to Boston. Seven hours of testing, with a specialist so well-known his name came up when one searched the term "Stargardt Disease," revealed that indeed, Eli had it.

"No, no, nothing neurological here. He's *just* losing his vision."

I took a full breath for the first time in a month.

"That we can handle!" I remember thinking.

Starting in Boston, we began learning all we could about Stargardt Disease. It's a recessive inherited retinal disease that causes the loss of central vision and leads to legal blindness. Most people diagnosed retain some peripheral vision, so while it's not currently treatable or curable, there are great tech tools that help with magnification. In short, if you can make things bigger, the blind spot in the middle of Eli's visual field covers up less of what he's trying to see. I became his advocate and was confident we had managed the pivot with grace.

My dear friend and boss asked me, "Are you sure you are ok? You say you are, but really, I don't know how you can be."

I assured him I was.

After all, we had a better path from the potential diagnoses.

Eli was handling the news in stride and making all the bad puns.

Sharing a souvenir from the retinal camera in Boston, "Oh, you got an iPod for Christmas? I got an eye picture!"

We were doing awesome… weren't we?

No is Often an Invitation to Yes

It was six weeks after diagnosis when I found myself frantically searching for my son inside our house when he should have been safely tucked in his bed.

Eli padded up the stairs with a bewildered look on his face.

At some point in the middle of the night, Eli woke up, and instead of coming upstairs to find us, he went into his little sister's tiny room and curled up on the floor of the smallest closet in the whole house.

My heart burst into a thousand pieces.

This poor boy sought comfort on the floor over finding his parents.

Clearly, we were not managing as well as I wanted to believe.

Starting work that day, I called my boss. "I need your help. You were right. Things are hard and I can't travel anymore. I'll do anything for work, but I can't be on the road for sales."

He compassionately said, "Give me two weeks. We'll figure this out."

And true to his word, he did.

Within days, my boss called and said "I have a project that needs to be managed for a new educational product. You'll oversee the writing of the curriculum and manage the timelines. I know you don't have experience, but I think you'll be good at it. If I give you this project and reduce your territory by half, will that work?"

I was sold–and grateful. I could be home more to support the needs of my family as we navigated Eli's diagnosis. What could have easily ended a thirteen-year career with a company I loved, was instead an invitation to deepen my skills. I didn't know then, but this project would change my life.

As I said "yes" to a new work opportunity, my family leaned into creating "visual memories" while Eli could file them away for safe keeping as his vision continued to erode.

We took road trips to National Parks and went on drives to find jackalopes. We spent time at the aquarium in Chicago and felt the July heat in New Orleans. We didn't plan a lot. We didn't save up; we simply went. We didn't use electronics during the day- except in Kansas– where some quick math determined you could see 40 miles away. That's a lot of corn and soybeans!

And thanks to my new role, I was editing math problems in the front seat of our truck as the girls played the license plate game in the back, and Eli colored in the map.

Our new family balance was great, and I traveled to a national conference for work that winter. My new work project led to others and sparked a keen interest in curriculum creation and design. I listened to our Chief Learning Officer describe the fields of Learning Science and Learning Engineering. He explained how learning was measurable and how learning design followed the same process I learned as an undergraduate in engineering and then physics. I could barely sit still.

A nudge deep in my soul said, "This is it. Say yes."

This was the next step in my career.

I met with my boss at the end of the presentation. He knew my heart wasn't in sales anymore. I enthusiastically told him I was going back to school to study Learning Science.

He smiled broadly, "You'll be great at that."

Within three months, I was enrolled.

Hold Space for Others

Eli was thriving with a great support team at school as I enrolled in an online program for Instructional Design and Technology with a focus on adult education. I was fortunate to work in a large educational company where my school projects turned into real improvements for our students. However, as my studies wound down, I began looking for a new internal role where I could combine my degree with my experience and leverage my relationships to help the company. In addition, the hybrid job created for me wasn't working for the company anymore, and my new boss was going to cut it entirely.

I had a phone meeting with our VP for Learning and Data Science, John

THE WHAT NOW MINDSET

Harnisher, Ph.D. We hit it off, but he had no open positions and loosely said he'd stay in touch.

The yearly budgets were finalizing, and as I feared, my hybrid job was not funded for the year.

I nervously emailed John.

I heard nothing back for weeks.

What I couldn't have known was that John had been angling to ensure I had a seat on his team. Days before the deadline, I traveled to Upstate NY and had a virtual meeting with John. When he screen-shared, the job description appeared. It was my dream job. I was going to be the first trained instructional designer to sit on John's Learning Science team.

He truly could have hired anyone for this role, as our large company was well-known in the educational space. While he *could* have had anyone, he *wanted* me. What's more, John made sure I was successful in my new role. He would often tell me that I was the voice of the learner, and he would back me on any evidence-based decision I made. Had I gone to work for any other company, my prior experience- in sales- would have been seen as irrelevant. Instead, my long tenure was seen as a benefit to John, who knew I could get buy-in from my colleagues. Which, thanks to his support, is exactly what happened.

When I look back, it's easy to see if Eli had not been diagnosed with Stargardt Disease, I never would have changed careers. That change was shepherded by leaders who saw my potential and held space for me to safely accelerate my career. I try to do the same for the team I now lead and am gently reminded of how it all started with a decision to not worship the thorn. Oh, and to always say "yes" to a jackalope hunt.

ABOUT
KRISTIN MURNER

Kristin Murner is a practitioner of learning design, a seasoned speaker, an advocate for inherited retinal disease research, a persistent runner, and the most compliant physical therapy patient ever. Late to appreciating that learning is a science, Kristin pivoted careers after more than a decade in medical and nursing educational sales to instructional product creation. While she has experience in K-12, for-profit and traditional higher-ed, professional development and corporate training, her passion is solidly for the underdog in all of those groups. Kristin is a firm believer that trials expose opportunities to learn new ways of doing things, and is dedicated to helping others do exactly that in the classroom, the workplace and in life. She holds a BS in Physics, an MBA in Marketing, and an MSEd in Instructional Design and Technology.

ABOUT THE WHAT NOW MOVEMENT

The What Now Movement seeks to create an international community of entrepreneurs, authors, and career professionals who gather for the purpose of innovation, collaboration, and for the sharing of resources and ideas. It is our belief that if we partner together to build this community, we undoubtedly will be more productive individually as well as collectively.

WNM Ventures, LLC is the formal business entity of The What Now Movement. Headquartered in Lanham, Maryland, it is a small, minority-owned business that has a network of over 100 subject matter experts worldwide in the following core business areas: Education support, marketing & communications, professional and management development, management consulting, and diversity and inclusion.

WNM Ventures delivers on both virtual and in-person platforms. The caliber of subject matter experts we provide, our experience in the core business areas, and our understanding of the federal and private sector, are the factors that set us apart from the competition.

We begin the process by working closely with our customers to understand the unique challenges they face to ensure we are providing services that address the specific needs of the organization.

Eric M. Twiggs, President & Chief Executive Officer

Ted Fells, Vice-President & Chief Strategy Officer

Dr. Sharon H. Porter, Vice-President & Chief Media & Communication Officer

Dawn Marie Bornheimer, Chief Movement Officer

Maisha B. Hoye, Chief Marketing Officer

Made in the USA
Middletown, DE
22 August 2023

37185031R00060